WHO'S ROWING YOUR BOAT?

BUILDING ADMINISTRATIVE TEAMS

Michelle E. Small

All Websites and other links are referenced at the end of the book.

Published by Kingz Publishing

Sandy Springs, GA

ISBN: 978-0-578-79112-8

Dedication

To my family,

Thank you for your love and support,

every time I launched into the deep.

You all are the iron that sharpened my life.

TABLE OF CONTENTS

Forward

If you are a leader, then read this book. Whether you manage corporation or non-profit, *Who's Rowing Your Boat* is a keep safe. Alleviate the stress of finding the candidate, or who's the best at executing vision. Each chapter provides insight on how to create the ideal administrative team. Secondly, it highlights the components of a dual relationship–Leader and Administrator, and Administrator and team. Finally, all the experiences provided by the author is practical and timeless, "servant-leadership" is an art that has long been misunderstood. At the completion of this work, you and your team will be made better.

Pastor Tyrell J. Murray, MBA

Introduction

The US Rowing's senior national team represents the U.S. at the highest level of international competition at either the Olympic Games or world championships. These athletes also compete at the Rowing World Cups and the Pan American Games.

The University of Washington rowing has produced a total of 73 Olympians in its history. UW had 12 rowers at the 2012 London Olympics, the most Huskies ever at Olympic Games. The 12 combined to win seven medals – one gold, three silver, and three bronze – to run UW's total to 42 Olympic medals, including 23 gold medals.

Successful rowing crews operate as a unit, moving together so as not to upset the balance of the boat and slow it down. There may be some famous names in a crew, but, unlike football and rugby, there are no star performers; no one oarsman will win a race through individual performance. But that does not mean that each member of the boat does not have an important, and slightly different, role to play. Oarsmen are faced away from the direction they are traveling, the front of the boat is inhabited by Bow, but it is at the back of the boat or the stern where you find the voice. (Meet The Teams)

CHAPTER 1

THE ADMINISTRATIVE TEAM—YOUR CREW!

A row team is called a crew. A crew consists of rowers and a coxswain, also known as the cox. The rowers in a crew sit with their backs to the bow or front section of the boat. The rowers provide the propulsion via their use of oars. In a crew of eight, the rowers are further split into technical-class rowers. There are those who keep the boat stable and balanced, and those who are the powerhouse are in the middle, providing strength and power. There are those who are at the stern, where the management duties are held. Then, there is the stern, which holds the Coxswain or Cox who has the responsibility of steering and motivating the team during the race.
(The Beginners Guide to Rowing, 2017)

You, Leader, Executive, Pastor, and Entrepreneur need a team...you need a crew. Your vision, business, or or ministry may not need a full crew immediately, but you will need one eventually. One of the top reasons why new businesses struggle or fail early is because the visionary, the leader, the executive, or the pastor attempts to do everything by themselves. The truth is that you cannot do and should not try to do everything by yourself. You cannot be the visionary, strategist, travel agent, media specialist, and IT professional at the same time. There was a time when one person starting could do it all, but in this day of fast-paced technology, going at it alone is no longer feasible, nor is it cost-effective. That would be equal to attempting to join a rowing competition, with a rowboat. The need for an administrative team is no longer just a consideration for large organizations' executives. Any individual with a vision, a purpose, and a plan to implement, needs an administrator or a team. If you are an entrepreneur, you may believe, "it's just me right now," oblivious to the fact that your vision will become larger, and a team will be needed at some point in time. Right now, you may be in a rowboat, and that's okay when you are just beginning. As we begin this journey together, take a moment now to sit in your boat, look at where you want to go, who you need, or most importantly, which skillsets will you need to get you were you want to go? You may not be in the position to hire an eight-man crew, and that is okay for now, but you should have an idea of what that eight-person crew would look like. If you want to compete on the world stage, if you want to experience a strong forward movement, then hiring the right administrator and an effective administrative team will be critical for your success.

CHAPTER 2

LIFE'S TRAINING, MY JOURNEY

From outside the rowing world, coxswains are usually thought of as small yelling machines that count every stroke. From inside the rowing world, coxswains are known for their ability to read what's going on in the boat, to steer, to motivate, and to sometimes make the calls that can win or lose the race.
(Secret training behind rowing's top coxswains 2019.)

I was invited to speak at a leadership business forum, and as usual, the facilitator requested my biography or in some circles, it is called a "one-sheet." That one piece of paper that lists all your accomplishments, hoping it conveys to the audience you might know something about that which you are speaking about. I would generally drop my head during the reading, praying that it's not read in its entirety. No such luck, the entire bio was read, but this time, I paid attention to my own story. Dates, professional titles, awards given, and certifications received all captured in the journey of forty years of work history. Yet, biographies are black and white statements of facts, but so much of the best parts of our life experiences are lived in the spaces in-between the words. These spaces between the lines hold several successes, adversities, life-long friendships, and the internal perseverance learned on this journey.

I would like to pause now and encourage you, write out your journey. Not the story you give to the ghostwriter to perfect, but the details in-between the lines of your resume. Write it out as a memorial of perseverance for yourself and as a guidepost for others to follow.

My journey through the corporate experience started when I began working for a large telecommunications company in Thousand Oaks, California, as a long-distance operator. Let me explain for this generation. Back in 1983, to place a long-distance call, you needed to dial zero on your telephone (no time to describe a rotary phone), and an operator would plug into a large board, answering with, "Operator, how may I help you?" Yes, we have come a long way baby! Working as an operator, sitting side by side with other operators, is where I have developed long-term relationships and friendships that I have until this day. Being that an operator was a 24-hour a day profession, we had different shifts that we could sign-up. The best shifts were based on seniority. Those with the lowest seniority were usually stuck with the worse shift called the 12-hour split-shift. This split-shift was 8 am – 12 pm, off four hours, then return to work 4 pm – 8 pm. Yes, it was that horrible, and at times, it felt unfair as they had me locked down for 12 hours a day. Even when I was off for those 4 hours, I was aware that my day was not over.

After working as, a Long-Distance Operator, I received a transfer to the Special Services Department. This department was responsible for designing different types of telecommunication circuits; this was long before fiber optics. During this assignment, I was appointed to receive special security clearance to work on secured circuits known as the White House Authorized Communications Circuits (WACA) for President Ronald Reagan and his staff. When then-President Reagan came to his ranch house in Santa Barbara, California, I worked directly with the Secret Service to activate the ranch house's telephone lines. While working with the Secret Service agents, I was invited to watch Air Force One take off from the military base, "Sure." I said, it would mean a day off. He asked for my name and date of birth, and pow! He knew everything about me, my address, marital status, everything. When I arrived on the military base, I realized this was not an offer extended to everyone. The moment President Ronald Reagan arrived at the military base, it went on lock-down. I can't share everything I experienced, but our United States Secret Service is fantastic. I am sure I no longer have that clearance, but I am equally sure I am in the system somewhere.

One of the advantages of working for a major corporation is the vast experiences one can obtain without leaving the company. I left the Special Services department when I was promoted to the position of a Customer Service Advisor (CSA). In this position, I was teamed up with an account executive to provide customer service support for some of the company's top-tiered clients. Over time, the company I worked for merged with another telecommunications company. With this merger, jobs were eliminated, and new positions were created. My position changed to include the role of a Database Analysis (DBA), with the increased duties of on-site data collection, engineering, and customer training.

My client base ranged from small legal firms in Brentwood, California, to major companies such as American Airlines, Wolfgang Puck, Bank of America, and FBI offices throughout Southern California. I also worked at California Prisons, Police departments, and the Los Angeles Unified School System. To work on school campuses, all employees had to be finger-printed. During my career, I have been examined by the Secret Service and fingerprints registered with the Department of Justice, so guess who is not running from the police? My position as a CSA/DBA required me to go to customers' sites, become familiar with their operation, and to address their telecommunication needs. After the programming was complete, I would return to administer on-site training for their employees and specialized training for their administrators. In the early nineties, I was not interested in programming or engineering communication systems, and I hadn't seen many women in that field. As a CSA/DBA, my immediate supervisor, who was a woman, was determined to see that I received certification for every communication system that the company sold. This field was male-dominated, and often, I was the only woman in the room receiving the training. Yet, because of her, I became certified in at least 13 or 14 different telecommunications systems.

Today, we should be thankful and support organizations like *Girls that Code.* These organizations promote coding and programming for girls. Thirty years ago, these organizations did not exist for young girls or women. Encouragement had to come from mentors that could see the possibilities in you. There is a scripture that says, *"As iron sharpens iron, one man sharpens another."* I am thankful for the "*iron*" that has sharpened me throughout my career, and I will highlight them throughout this book. What is most interesting about my training, certifications, and experiences is that I did not have a desire to learn programming or coding, as it is called today, but oh, for the "iron!"

Every assignment and every interaction with my customer base was always viewed as an opportunity to grow. On one particular assignment, I was assigned to train a well-known celebrity in her home, and I did not know who it was until I arrived. Once I entered her home, what impressed me the most was not her fame or beauty; but she wanted to learn how to do the programming herself. She had a full staff that could have done it for her. To this day, I remember the way she looked at me in the middle of training and said, "*keep doing what you are doing.*" At that moment, I thought she meant programming her system; later, I realized it was so much more. That woman was the iconic Dianna Ross, and she became another piece of "*iron*" in my life.

I had many more experiences like this, and I have been fortunate to have met people from all backgrounds, ethnicities, races, and industries, and I have used everything that I've learned throughout my journey. I retired from that company after 19 years of service. Armed with skills, certifications, and a great deal of confidence, I successfully opened my own business as a programmer and a trainer. Then, life happened. Life happens always! I found myself in a divorce and in need of a new start in a new location. Packing up my belongings, my company, and my pride, I left California behind, and I headed to Georgia. Starting over in a new state, I knew I needed income, so I signed up with a temporary staffing agency in hopes of finding a position in programming or engineering. When I did receive a call from the agency, the employment opportunity was not for engineering position, but the request was to fill a temporary position as an executive assistant. The job entailed assisting a high-maintenance executive who had already gone through two assistants. The agency felt my personality and temperament would be a good match, and this assignment was only until an engineering position became available. This position was with the local newspaper, and I recognized a pattern. First telecommunications, and now newspapers, a different form of media, but media nonetheless. "Sure," I said, why not since, it was only temporary, and I had been around this mountain of media before. After working with this vice president for 15 days, he called me into his office. "*Do you like it here?*" He asked, and I was confused and sure he was about to fire me. I told him I did, and he said, "*I want you to work for me permanently.*" I reminded him that as a temporary employee, I must be on assignment for six months before becoming released from my contract. "*Don't worry, let me handle that.*" This executive paid a lot of money to buy me out of that contract because he did not want to lose me. Please note, I did not have experience as an administrative assistant, nor did I desire to be one. I asked him to give me a day to think about it. In prayer, I asked God about my direction, and He let me know that if I can coordinate systems, then I can coordinate people. And that was my entry into becoming an administrative assistant to a vice president.

How did I know I could do this position and do it well? Because of my personal crew. I learned the importance of having quality friends early in my life. Quality, by my definition, are individuals, both men and women, who are passionate and focused on their goals. These set of people are equally passionate about pushing me to reach my goals; who will not only comfort me on those days when comfort is needed, but who know me well enough to push me when I do not want to get out of bed. These are those "*iron*" people I referenced earlier. Too often, when someone is blessed to have an 'iron' person in their life, they reject them. Why? Because iron people can and often do hurt. Not to destroy you, but to sharpen you. People say they want to be sharpened, but they only allow what I call "butter knife people" close to them. A butter knife won't sharpen anything! All a butter knife can do is spread stuff. I am grateful for all of the "*iron*" individuals that have crossed my path, and I pray I have been an iron to others.

I love God, and I am thankful for those people He has given me throughout my life. Because I am a woman of faith, this book is composed of many timeless spiritual truths that have guided me in my life. There have been individuals of all faiths who have seen something in me and encouraged me along the way. People may think they can succeed without having anyone speak into their lives, which might be true. But this life journey is so much easier if you follow wisdom's counsel. "*Without good direction, people lose their way; the wiser the counsel you follow, the better your chances*". *Proverbs 11:14. MSG*

Whatever leadership position you find yourself in, whether the leader of a large company, a pastor of a medium-sized church, or the CEO of your own business, you most likely already have an administrative assistant, or you know you need to hire one quickly. In reading this book, you will understand the need for hiring excellent administrative assistants and the importance of creating strong administrative teams; your crew. The first position we need to identify for your team is the role of the administrator; your Coxswain.

CHAPTER 3

PREP FOR THE COXSWAIN

A great coxswain embodies specific traits, has an exceptional grasp on the skills needed in coxing, and adds a dash of magic to become an indispensable member of the crew. A cox is: Positive, Intelligent, Confident, Selfless, and Competitive. Through hard work and practice, they can communicate clearly with purpose and authority. They can steer and maneuver a shell-like boat as an extension of their own person; they have a strong understanding of the mechanics of the rowing stroke and the propulsion of a shell; they know how to relate to and motivate people in a positive way, unifying them to achieve their best; they can read real-time events before they happen, and adjust to achieve the desired results both in practice and during a race.
(The Down and Dirty Guide to Coxing, 2019)

Administrative assistant, executive assistant, secretary, and administrative professional; this title has changed multiple times over the years, along with its expected responsibilities. Whatever term you chose to call these professionals, one thing has not changed over time; to run an efficient organization, one must seek the right person to fill this position. Throughout this book, you may hear these titles used interchangeably. Some of the reasons leaders cite when looking for an administrator is; to help me stay organized, to assist me with correspondence, both electronic and physical, to answer phone calls, respond to voice messages, and the ever-popular "I don't know, I just need help." All of these needs are valid, and yes, you do need the help. The number one most important reason for hiring an administrator or an administrative team is because you cannot do, and should not try to do everything yourself! The second most important consideration when hiring an administrator is to keep the leader on his goals. As the leader, if you believe you alone can produce your vision, stay committed to your schedule, and keep your boat moving, you will fail. Not necessarily in your business, but in your productivity and effectiveness. Unfortunately, when the leader is in charge of their schedule, their minds, emotions, and life will often get in the way. It's the administrator's responsibility and pleasure to take care of, and take over your schedule for you. Like the Coxswain on the rowing team, the administrator does not have an oar in the water. They are the one facing forward, giving (actually yelling, shouting, squalling) to the team the directions and information needed to row effectively. At the other end of the boat is the bow, which provides balance to the boat and whose oar hits the water first, as they are the leader. The bow, with their back to the direction the boat is moving, trusts its crew's rowing skills and the voice of the Coxswain. Experience has shown, when the visionary oversees their calendar, a whole day can be lost, and it's usually in the mundane, not the productive. When your administrator is in charge of your schedule, they can lock it down by handling those responsibilities that do not add productivity to your day. An administrator becomes skilled at anticipating your needs. They know what their executive likes or dislikes, and they become proficient at handling your business with the same heart, intention, and voice as you. When you finally hire your administrator, you must make it a priority to communicate your goals and priorities, both corporately and personally. Because your priorities become their priorities, this is what's essential to an excellent administrator, learning all they can to take the load off you, which ultimately ensures your organization (or boat) moves smoothly.

One of the understated reasons for the hiring of an administrator is that they provide consistent support. When you are on the road, in meetings, or with your family, you have someone to support you consistently. I worked for a media company supporting various executives, sometimes three or four executives at one time. At any given moment, I could have executives in multiple states, yet I knew exactly where they were at all times. These executives had access to me, knowing I was a phone call or a text away. They also knew they probably could not reach me until after seven o'clock on Sundays. If one of the executives was in Houston and I learned of a tornado in that area, I knew that I had to stop what I was doing, then make airline and transportation reservations to get him back home safely. After that, I would return to my life as a mother, sister, minister, entrepreneur, and an administrator of a non-profit organization. It was working those 12-hour split-shifts as a long-distance operator that prepared me for this.

CHAPTER 4

SERVANT LEADERSHIP VS. TRANSFORMATIONAL LEADERSHIP

When you speak of an administrator or an administrative team, you are speaking of servant-leadership. The servant-leader is a servant; first, one with a natural, conscientious choice to assist or support a leader as the leader is leading others. This individual is sharply different from one who is a leader first or desires to lead within an organization. Servant leaders are usually so good at their profession that their reputation proceeds them. It is imperative to understand leadership styles when selecting your team. Traditional leadership, also known as "transactional leadership," is an individual that desires to be at the forefront, their employees produce through objectives, rewards, and punishments. In contrast with the transactional leader, is the transformational leader. These leaders inspire, direct, and motivate the team for the good of the organization. Then we have the servant leader. The servant leader, much like the transformation leader, will inspire, direct, and motivate, but their focus is their leader not the organization as a whole. This distinction is significant and must be closely identified. It has often been found that administrative professionals with a transactional temperament were placed in roles requiring the servant leader. Whether the individual is a transactional leader or a transformational leader, for a true servant-leader, the team is not their focus, you the leader will be their focus. When interviewing one with the character of a transformational leader, you may hear, "*I really like and admire you as a leader, and I can learn from you*" or "*I really like the way you operate, and I want to be like you.*" This statement is flattering and sounds nice, but they're not a true servant leader. If you select this person to be your administrator, they will be with you long enough to glean from you before they move on. Now, you the leader will be wondering why pieces of your organization have left with them; leaving you with trust issues the rest of your team will have to deal with. We will cover more on trust later. A true servant leader wants to serve you as you produce your vision. In an interview, the first question they may ask you is, "*May I see your calendar?*"

The second will be, "*What are your personal goals?*" Why is that important? Because an administrator will never handle your professional schedule at the expense of your personal schedule. In short, there is a difference between someone filling a position within your organization and someone whose passion to partner with the leader to fulfill their vision.

CHAPTER 5

CHARACTERISTICS (PERSONALITIES) OF THE CREW

Coxswain: *I'll pass on the leadership stuff, Napoleon complex garbage, and point out a secondary character or two that coxes unintentionally inherit after riding in the box for a while. They cannot drive a car anymore. They take 10 miles to change a lane, oversteer, cannot find the brakes, and yell to the car a lot. This has nothing to do with the coxswain's former driving ability. Coxes also squint a lot, no loss in vision, they just squint.*

Stroke or seat eight: *The meekest, most frightened non-rower in the world; when plugged in reluctantly in the stroke seat, stays meek up until the first few strokes. The first few strokes, a thought grows in the wimps' sniveling little mind that this job is his/hers for life. Strokes are born and made to be the most competitive persons in the boat by far, and if they stroke long enough,* *become overly competitive in everything they pursue, or don't pursue.*

***Seven:** I don't know if whining, overly bossy, and big-mouthed complainers are born, and I can't believe that the cosmic effect of this seat could possibly be so instantaneous. The longer one rows at seven, the more sophisticated and complex the "complaining" becomes.*

***Six:** The gentle giant, the gorilla in the mist. Six absorbs most of Seven's "complaining" and keeps it from moving through to the rest of the crew. Six nods and agrees a lot. It is a hard thing for a normal person to row Six. Sixes are characterized by great competence in the execution of rowing and life, but they exhibit poor self-confidence and a propensity to self-flagellation.*

***Five:** God. Yahweh. Allah. Buddha. It's not that the five seat IS those things, it's just that's how (s)he gets treated. If a photo is taken of the crew, five will look great, everyone else is caught with shirttails out. Five is an example of what happens to a bum that is treated like a king; they act like one. The fortunate thing is that the unearned unabashed worship lasts only as long as the time on the water.*

***Four:** The Amnesia-seat. Fourth seat is not stupid, it just has immediate and catastrophic memory loss. Four will forget to tell the boatman about his(her) stripped rigger nut - usually from the time he is told by the coach until he arrives at the boatman's bench, wondering what he is doing there. On that first day on the water, as the ice is breaking up, who is rummaging around the back of the boathouse looking for a sweatshirt? Four is why racing shirts are handed out on a race day.*

***Three:** Late in the water. Late to practice. Late to class. Late to work. Late out of the water. Late to his date. Late to the team bus. Late for everything but the chow line. Three generally gets assigned a sitter. Two: Lean to the left, lean to the right, stand up, sit down, fight, fight, and fight. The Cheerleader. What* *is amazing as seven is whining about the balance, the spacing, no swing, and rushing: Two is back there with pom-poms saying: ALL RIGHT GUYS! LET'S DO THAT AGAIN!*

***Bow:** Comedian. The bow seat creates a strange fatalism. They know that in a catastrophic collision, they will be the only one to die or get paralyzed. Consequently, there is a constant quiet stream of one-liners that two or three could probably hear if two were not cheering loudly. Note: I didn't write this, I just think it's hilarious. No offense meant.*

(Rowingsoundsfun, 2012)

Every member of your crew must have their individual purpose. And with having a unique purpose, they will also have unique personalities. Like the crew of a rowing team, all the personalities may be different, but they are all necessary for the position they are responsible. As often with the administrative assistant, the Coxswain may appear controlling, negative, bossy, and unapproachable to those outside the boat. This personality type is what it takes when your team is in a race, a project, or a deadline. If you allow personal insecurities or voices outside of the boat to silence your Coxswain's voice, you may experience your boat slowing or coming to a complete stop. The stroke or seat eight is well prepared to handle the constant orders coming from the Coxswain. This person depends on it the most! If the team slows down or misses a deadline, they will blame the Coxswain for not keeping them informed. Seat seven is much like seat eight, but they will not directly confront the administrative assistant on missed deadlines.

Seat seven will follow up with seat eight; not that they are divisive, they just work better with eight, slightly removed from the constant commands. Seat six, five, and four are your power seats. Technology, finance, and marketing; these three keep your boat moving, and they know it. They are excited to help but seated where any errors will not stop the team's forward movement. Seat two is needed in most organizations, but many do not realize their importance. This person is a combination of cheerleader, event planner, and keeper of all things fun. This is the person who plans the company party, organizes the after five, events, and has a list of all the members' birthdays. Unfortunately, many believe this is the administrative assistant's responsibility, with all the other duties to keep the team moving. I mean, really? If there is no assigned seat within the team, the administrator will usually fill this spot by outsourcing it. Problem solved.

Seat two. Calm, not easily rattled, seat two is often the closest to the leader, and this is why they can be the back-up for the stroke. They have a seat close enough to the leader to understand the purpose and flow of the boat. Together, the number two person and the bow provide balance for the team. Sometimes, the bow will appear as if they do not take the race seriously, with jokes, stories, and laughter! Why? Because they trust their team. Just Relax.

You may not be able to hire eight different individuals right now. Some of these responsibilities may be combined, but what is most important is to realize that a person with a unique personality or one that is different from yourself should not be discounted from your team. It is your responsibility as the leader to place the right character in the right position.

Where personalities and positions may differ, over time, I have identified three critical characteristics to look for when hiring those individuals that will make up your crew. It is easy to remember...time, talent, and trust.

CRITICAL CHARACTERISTICS —TIME

Split time: In rowing, there is seemingly nothing as important as a faster split time. Generically shown as your pace per 500m, your split time is the best accountability metric you have – the lower it goes, the harder you are working. Like most important things in life, getting your split time low (and keeping it there) can be challenging. Especially for those that are new to rowing, controlling your split time can be both frustrating and confusing. While you may feel like you are rowing harder, you may actually be going slower.
(A Faster Rowing Split Time: 4 Tips You Can't Forget! 2019)

Time; the first and most critical characteristic in choosing your administrator. When choosing an administrator or an administrative team, you must first ascertain if they know the value of time. Time is the most valuable resource for any leader. There are only two things that I know God is not making more, "land and time." If that is the case, we all need to be better stewards over both. An administrator must understand all that you're dealing with and what's critical to your success. When armed with this knowledge, they can ensure their leader is focused on the high-leverage activities, and they will decline or delegate the rest. They are aware that one unplanned event can throw off an entire day, and as the saying goes, "time is money." It is the administrator's responsibility to master your calendar. In all areas of life, leaders live and die by the calendar. Deadlines, appointments, meetings, presentations, calls—the calendar is your flight plan that keeps all your moving parts from crashing into each other, including personal commitments that often take place during working hours. If your administrator doesn't have mastery of your entire calendar, you do not have a servant leader administrator.

In my position as an executive assistant, I managed two to four executives at a time. Each executive had a different requirement for me. Exec-A only wanted me to handle his travel as he maintained his calendar. Exec-B & C gave me the ability to view their calendars, backing them up in case of an emergency, and Exec-D was my "full-service" executive. Managing his calendar required me to know his schedule, starting from one hour before he was to be in the office for his first meeting until his day ended, not the end of the day.

Throughout the workday, his schedule was packed with meetings. I knew what time a meeting began and where the meeting would take place. This type of calendar oversight was not done the night before or the day of; I worked the calendar at least two – three weeks prior. I have often been asked how and why you would schedule the calendar a month in advance; I asked, "How could you not?" When I began working with a new executive, they didn't always feel comfortable giving me total control of their calendar, which was understandable if they had not worked with an executive assistant previously. Once trust (that I knew what I was doing) was established, I received full control of his calendar, and a new process began. I created something called "hold time," consisting of 30 minutes or an hour blocks of time on the calendar. This was their time allowance, which I cautioned them to spend wisely. If they chose to give away that block of time for a meeting because they ran into someone that needed a meeting while in the restroom, that time was gone, and he was not getting any more. As I previously said, time is a resource, and we are not getting more of it. After running out of their 'time-allowance" a few times, it was understood, with even greater importance, the need of totally relinquishing their calendar to me. An effective administrator is also skilled with prioritizing personal time. If your administrator defaults to prioritizing the professional time at the expense of your personal time, they are not a servant leader – at least not yet. Protecting personal time maximizes professional time. An administrator must know your full calendar, which allows them to guard your time. When choosing an administrator or administrative team, as I said, they need to value time and be a good steward of time. Admittedly, are administrators' great managers of their own time? No! Because their talent is not in managing themselves, it is in managing their leader. My real talent was rendering service to those that I have been assigned to serve.

CRITICAL CHARACTERISTICS —TALENT

In the sport of rowing, each rower is numbered by their boat's position in ascending order from the bow to the stern.

Eight or Stroke. *The man who can best stand the punishment is the stroke, setting a pace that perhaps only he knows the crew will be able to maintain throughout the race. It is important that the rest of the crew stays with him and, over a course of this length, finding a steady rhythm is vital.*

Seven – Stroke's Lieutenant. *Seven has a vital support role to play. If he does not back-up the stroke's commitment, or follow any change in pace, it is certain that none of the rest of the crew will.*

Six, Five, Four – Power Team. *The middle four of the boat are the engine room. But, of the four, six is the brain of the operation, making sure the rhythm of the stern is not lost when it reaches the less subtle middle of the boat. Sixes are* *characterized by great competence in execution of rowing and life.*

Three – All boats have one. *The three seat is where the least technically able oarsman sits. He is not far enough towards the stern to upset the rhythm, but, as he is not right at the bow, any error will not result in the boat swerving.*

Two – Everyone need a Two. *Two is often the seat occupied by the back-up stroke. Two joins the man behind him to make up the Bow Pair who, with the first blades to catch the water at the front of the boat, must be the sharpest members of the crew at the beginning of the stroke.*

Bow – Keeps the boat balanced. *The bow joins Two in making sure that the boat is balanced correctly. As the man at the front of the boat, his blade makes the most difference when it is placed in the water, so he must be sharp and technically correct.*

(Gough, How the eight works, 2006.)

Talent matters! As your business advances, you will not only need an administrator, but you will also need to build an administrative team. The first step for all leaders is to have a clear understanding of what talents, needs, and requirements they are looking for from the team. Just like the rowing team, every member has their assigned position among the crew. Once the specification has been established, you need to know how to find this talent. One of the oldest means of finding a person or team of individuals is the use of a resume. Today, the resume is now uploaded into various online hiring platforms, and it is still the most requested tool when hiring. It is the resume that gets one in the door. If you are hiring an employee, an internship, or even if you are seeking volunteers for an unpaid position with a non-profit organization, the resume should still be requested. In looking for an administrator, the resume can determine an individual's skillset and flexibility. It will reveal if they possess the most critical skill; a servant's heart. Individuals who have supervised departments or were in charge of a group of people will have a challenge with not injecting their previous experience and opinions on your operation's workings. Even if their experience is excellent and their insight is spot on, remember that they are there for you, not so much for the organization. This is the key to hiring a superb administrator.

An administrator should also be skilled at creating and mastering systems. Whatever line of work you're in, effective performance depends on a certain number of set preferences and procedures. Do you know what works best for you and your team? An administrator will document and systematize what is essential to you, so you do not always reinvent the wheel. An administrative team has a set of personalized expertise. You must be comfortable knowing that they have the skills to do the job you require. Your team must know how to skillfully use the oars or tools given to them. Even though these individuals may not have leadership positions or governance areas within your organization, they are essential for your organization to function. This is not just a concern for the CEO of a large organization or the leader of a non-profit organization, but also the entrepreneur starting their own business. Do you need someone to help with emails? Do they know how to use distinctly different platforms, such as Microsoft Outlook, Gmail, or GoDaddy? If you need someone to assist with your marketing, do they know how to use popular social media platforms, such as LinkedIn, Instagram, or Facebook? Do they know how to track media trends using Google Analytics? These applications are tools that people use daily, and it's often assumed everyone knows how to use them. The resume is still the best starting point for accessing skills and choosing wisely. I'll give you an example of what could happen when you do not use a resume. I was responsible for overseeing a team of five individuals for a non-profit organization. There was a young woman I had observed for many months, and she was always on time, always professionally dressed, and she always had a pleasant and stable demeanor. I learned that she worked as a technical assistant. I brought her on the team, and part of her responsibility was to assist in organizing membership contact information. I needed her to update all the member's addresses, emails, and phone numbers. Everything was in an Excel spreadsheet for her to work on; again, I wanted to start her with something easy. After a week of not hearing from the young lady,

I contacted her to see how the task was coming along. Few days later, I followed-up, and to my surprise, she told me, "Well, I looked at the chart, and I couldn't figure it out." I said, "What couldn't you figure out?" She replied, "I even had a co-worker help me, and she couldn't figure it out either." Now, I was confused, since this was simply updating a spreadsheet, then it dawned on me, so I finally asked, "Do you know how to use Microsoft Office?" And she said, "No, we don't have that at work. We work on dedicated machines with pre-loaded applications." Well, the spreadsheet was color-coded by department, with pivot tables and everything. But I never asked the woman if she had this skillset, and I never asked for a resume. I did try to work with her to learn Excel, but since she had never known any part of Microsoft office, she could not grasp an Excel spreadsheet.

When you are building the team, you must be clear about what your requirements are. Do you just want to have a person who is present, accountable, and faithful? Or do you need specific skillsets for your organization to function? When looking for volunteers or non-paid interns, you still need to request a resume. In a business, if an assistant is hired and they are not skilled in doing the job you require, you let them go. But if you're in a ministry or a non-profit organization, most likely, the individual has an emotional connection and is passionate about working with you. Now, you're dealing with emotions, heart, and feelings. If it is a church, you may end up with a disgruntled member. If it's a non-profit organization, you may lose strong financial support, so you have to be cautious. Dr. Samuel Chand of "Dream Releaser Coaching" argues in his leadership training, "*you don't find talent from volunteers, you find talent from recruiting.*" When you have a project or building a team, you cannot just say, "I'm looking for volunteers who want to volunteer their time to help us." You may create the added trouble of finding work for individuals who answered the call but were not equipped. Remember, I stated that individuals who previously supervised departments or a group of people will have a challenge not injecting their prior experience into their work. Here is an example: One of the positions on an administrative team is the receptionist. A team I worked with had a lovely receptionist. She carried-out the typical reception tasks, greeting visitors, answering the phones, and taking messages. One day, a co-worker received an email from her, and it was four paragraphs long. It was a simple phone message that turned into who the caller was, what he wanted, and what we could do to solve his problem. We tried to tell her, "Dear, just write down his name and phone number," but we didn't because she was such a lovely person. Later, after reading her resume, we found out that she had a degree in Creative Writing and Literature. After the lovely lady was promoted to a position that honed her creative writing skills, we acquired another receptionist. This time, the requirements changed: Greet customers, answer the main phone line, and transfer to the appropriate department. The new receptionist was kind and articulate on the phone, professional in appearance, and courteous to our clients. One day, she had to send emails to the department because the voicemails system was down. Her writing was so bad; it took two of us to interpret what she was trying to say. For her, we had to say, "Don't write out messages, just come by, and verbally give us the message." Here are two different types of situations that a careful review of a resume would have given us a clue of what to expect from them. Know who your people are. Some people are great in one thing, and some are better for other things. It doesn't wipe someone out from being part of the team; you just need to know which skills work on your team. Like a rowing crew's different personalities, you will have personalities and skillsets that vary in your crew. As the leader, it is your responsibility to determine who sits in what seat and who can hold a seat until it is their time. This is true for most of the crew's seats, except the Coxswain seat, and only one person can fill this role.

There was a time when many believed all they needed was one trusted administrative assistant. That one person would be responsible for holding trusted information for booking travel or scheduling conferences. This person would also be accountable for information such as the leader's full legal name, date of birth, passport numbers, and credit card numbers for both the leader, and even at times, their spouse. One individual may be trustworthy at handling confidential matters, but may not be familiar with all functions, such as social media platforms. Many leaders shy away from social media, delegating it to their administrator, but what if they are not familiar with all forms of social media for businesses? Social media is no longer a personal choice, it has become the primary mode of communication for this generation. Once upon a time, I was unfamiliar with all social media platforms, and it was my daughter that forced me to start utilizing Instagram, of which I am now a semi-pro! However, one will quickly learn that managing all these platforms can take up an entire day. Even though it is time-intensive, many businesses soon learned that not having a social media presence is just as detrimental as poor representation. For a business to ignore social media is to ignore revenue, which means this function must be part of your administrative team. As I began stretching out in my own business, I understood that I needed help, so I asked my daughter; who had become a self-taught media guru. For a while, she assisted me by scheduling my media posts for 30 days. This was a blessing, but eventually, I needed to hire someone because, as the founder and CEO of "Alignment Media and Marketing," she was not going to keep working for free, nor will I let her. (Yes, this is a mom plug) As a leader, you must recognize the critical seats or positions needed for your organization, and staff them accordingly as you grow. I remember questioning a local pastor who was once an administrator before becoming a pastor; if her previous experience was more helpful in finding the right administrator. The answer was yes, and no. Yes, because she knew the skills needed to do the job. And no, because if the person she did hire was lacking in those skills, she found herself just doing the work. She acknowledged that by doing this, she wasn't allowing the person to grow in their position.

As the leader, she came to realize that just because she could do the work didn't mean she should. Another challenge the pastor mentioned was the expectation of the administrative assistant to handle things the way she did when she was the administrative assistant. There has to be a time and space for role development, not only for the administrator, but for the leader. I have found the most significant challenge for most leaders who once worked in a position as a servant leader transforming into the transformational leader that is now needed. I cannot say this enough to leaders, "because you can do it does not mean you should." Is it a good use of time for you to wait online an hour for the Airlines versus going through your email to answer correspondence that will bring in new business?

In the corporate arena, there are many tests available for teams to evaluate personality, occupational interests, work habits, and social perceptions. These tests assist in identifying the team's decision making process in their personal and professional lives. These tests, such as "The Birkman Test," are excellent tools for administrative teams and the leaders to take together. As an executive assistant, this test was very beneficial to me. I learned my style, which was similar to mine. This enabled me to know what kind of administrator or servant leader he/she needed me to be. Because a servant leader leads their leader from behind, it is imperative to know their personality type and leadership style. When working with multiple executives, I had to understand each of their personality types. One was laissez-faire and needed very little assistance. Another was high-strung, and I had to learn to keep the drama away from him without feeling out of control or disconnected from his team. Another executive was a combination of the two, and his expectation of me was to manage him completely. If he was in a meeting and another was starting, I had the responsibility of interrupting him and keeping him on his schedule. If there was a problem within his organization of an administrative nature, I did not bring him the issue without bringing him a solution. Yes, that was a lot! I didn't have to change hats at the beginning and end of each day; I changed hats at the entrance to each executive's office, all in the same day. Where did I get training for this? The school of life; back to my training as a CSA/DBA.

One of the top-tiered customers, a large airline company purchased a new system for their corporate office. Our regional director received word that they were very unhappy with the new phone system, and wanted it removed immediately. Before sending a technician to remove the system, which would result in the company losing the client, our director sent me. Arriving, I met our contact in the parking lot and asked what happened! I knew the telecommunications system quite well, it was easy to use, easy to program, and our top-selling product. As the liaison was giving me the feedback, I realized it was not the system. There was an apparent clash between the customer and the CSA/DBA assigned. Now,, to her credit she was very knowledgeable about this product, I know, because I trained her. But her personality type and her demeanor would have clashed with this customer because of culture.

When it comes to personal grooming, I believe two things; accessories should match, and black shoes don't go with everything. On this particular day, I had on my two-piece royal blue suit with gold buttons, bold gold earrings, bracelets, and broach. Topped off with a blue and yellow scarf to match. Pow! Runway programmer. But in the airport parking, all accessories were removed and placed in my purse, locked in the trunk. The liaison, who also was a woman, watched me with a bewildered look on her face as I told her, "Now I am ready." We entered the building, and I watched her tap on the client's door and immediately entered his office, however, I did not. I noticed his disapproving expression while she was explaining to him that someone was here to assist with the new telecommunications system. When he looked up and saw me standing in the doorway, he told me to enter. I entered, greeted him, and asked if I could come around to his side of the desk to examine the phone, and he said yes. I asked him, "What do you want this system to do?" He told me, I programmed it, stepped back around to the front of his desk, and asked if there was anything else. He smiled and said, "No, thank you." On the walk back to the car, my contact asked, "How did you win him over? He doesn't want anyone but you on-site?" I smiled and just said, "I am glad he is happy." Now, what was my superpower; understanding cultures and clothing.

"The formality of clothing might not only influence the way others perceive a person, and how people perceive themselves, but could influence decision making in important ways through its influence on processing style,". (When Clothing Style Influences Cognitive Style 2015)

What was my superpower? My grandmother. Myrtle L. Dunn, was a military wife, married to a Tuskegee Airman, Captain Charles Wesley Dunn and they lived among various cultures: England, Alaska, Utah and Japan. It was Japan that captivated her the most and it was her I developed my love for the Asian culture. One of my favorite movies is "The Last Samurai." It was from that movie I learned what Samurai means "servant or those who serve." And these are my life lessons: First, attire and mannerisms in business are different for different cultures. Japan is a country that takes both work and etiquette very seriously, it's probably not a surprise that Japanese business etiquette has a detailed code of proper conduct, all in an effort to foster an atmosphere of mutual respect and smooth cooperation. (10 Japanese Business Etiquette Rules, 2020). Through life experiences I have acquired a general business acumen. This is a crucial skill for every leader, the ability to foresee and break down complexities and uncertainties that surround business and people. In 2020, this generation believes that self-expression means not adapting to the environment or culture around you. "Be You, Do You" is the mantra of this generation. But my Bible tells me, "*I have become all things to all people so that by all possible means I might save some.*" Deferring to another's culture or personality does not decrease me, it increases me. It increased me greatly as I received a bonus from the account manager for saving his account.

Why is it essential for your administrator to know your leader's leadership style, personality type, and cultural mannerisms? Because administrators are your second brain. An administrator or administrative team will learn what you like and what you don't. They know where you are and where you need to be, both physically and mentally. They will learn when to schedule meetings and when not to. Your administrator knows when to give people access to you or when to block access. They will gather as much of this information as possible, as early as possible – to proactively keep you moving. This means excellent communication, both oral and written, are critical. Administrators often assist in facilitating communication in your organization – especially if bottlenecking happens in your organization. Whether it's emails, calls, or other communication, an administrator will accelerate response times from your team and keep things moving. Managing change is another essential skill of the administrator. Skilled administrators are experts in dealing with change. They don't mind it; actually, they accept it. Adapting to their leader's tendencies of change isn't a problem; it's just part of the fun in serving.

As the General Secretary of a non-profit, I have four administrators under me who all work for the organization's senior leaders, and I did not request volunteers. I observed how they handled many situations, then I asked for a resume. There are some on my team I have given assignments to, some I have not. This is that's due to the third critical characteristic; trust.

CHAPTER 8

CRITICAL CHARACTERISTICS —TRUST

(THE MOST CRITICAL)

The Cox: In Rowing, the coxswain is a vital addition to the crew. Besides steering, the cox is also the voice in the boat, coaxing, motivating, and calming an eight-man engine as the cox faces forward.
(Gough, How the eight works, 2006.)

Trust is a two-way street. A leader must have trust in their administrative team, and the team must trust that its leader has trust in them. Every important relationship begins and ends with trust. The trust between a leader, their administrator, and the team is most critical as they are also part of your inner circle. Looking at the example of the Coxswain at the back of the boat and the leader in the bow, the leader will feel the impact of a collision long before the rest of the crew. The one in the bow must fully trust in their Coxswain. An administrator handles your most confidential and sensitive company information, and they do respect your personal and the intimate. An administrator must be firm in integrity, with an acute sense of discretion. They have learned to be aware of people who are trying to get insider access or influence. When interviewing at the C-Suite level (Senior Executives, CEOs, CFO, and EVPs), the level of trust is higher. These executive assistants do not just hold your confidence but the confidence of the company. An experienced administrative assistant is aware that the interview process is not just for the executive to find the right assistant, but also for the assistant to partner with the right leader. A seasoned executive administrator is also aware that chemistry is even more important than any skill on the resume, because chemistry is connected to trust.

Every executive, CEO, or visionary needs one person they can trust with delegation. Knowing how to work basic office systems, keeping a calendar, or making travel reservations is the minimum requirement. At the executive level, it's a matter of trust, because you must feel confident in trusting the administrator with your time, goals, and vision.

Again, the hiring of an administrator is like hiring a second brain. Often, executives include their executive administrators in staff meetings, production meetings, and board meetings. Many executive administrators are granted or given delegated authority by their executives.

Once you have hired an administrator, the leader must take the time to sit down with them and lay out the organization's vision and, most importantly, your vision. This is critical to the administrator and the team because your vision becomes their "smart goals." If you don't communicate your vision and what is important to you, your administrator could end up working hard, and they could end up working hard against you. This is not because they are trying to be defiant, but because you haven't outlined clear expectations for you and your organization.

Why is it that so many leaders, especially those with small businesses or entrepreneurs, are so resistant to hiring an administrator or an administrative team? Because many fear losing control. It is terrifying to hand over your vision, all that you have put your heart, soul, and finances, into the hands of someone who's not even a co-owner. Leaders, if you've gone through the time and effort of recruiting, collecting resumes, hiring the perfect fit, and providing clear direction so that the vision is fully understood, trust and release those you set in place to do the job assigned. I can't say this enough; trust is a two-way street. As an executive administrator, I have often been accused of being controlled by those who had the ear of my leader, and they were right. I was controlling and committed to executing that which my leader had entrusted me with. A skilled administrator's most vital talent is not to get in front of their leader, but to lead from behind by perceiving their need and protecting this asset of trust. But to the leader, I say, the first person you must have trust in is yourself. Are you confident enough to allow the person and the team you put in place to row your boat as you have your back to the wind? In an article for the Harvard Business Review, Melba Dunkin wrote, "*Hiring the right administrative team can be a challenge. In some ways, it is trickier than filling a traditional management position because personal chemistry and the one on one dynamic is so important. Sometimes even more important than skills or experience when you're building an administrative team.*"

Remember the executive at the media company that paid a lot of money to buy me out of my contract, I later asked him, "Why did you choose me?" That was important to me because I was not a career administrator and I didn't have most of the other skills you would expect an executive assistant to have. He said something I will never forget; he said, "Because I trust you."

Conclusion

Over my 40+ year career, I would say that the most vital talent I have gained is speaking truth to power. I can look back at my resume now and see each position I worked; each person I met was actually a road sign to where I stand today. A career path that has had various experiences is one that qualifies you for now. Whether you are a leader or an administrator, again, I say "write out your story." Write your story, not the one eloquently written for LinkedIn, but the one that shows your ups and downs. Read it, then re-read it so you will remember what it was like to row the boat of another and what it is like to trust someone to row yours at the moment. A successful rowing team in competition is usually made up of eight members. Each position has trained well, and they know their position within the crew. Each member also understands the role and purpose of all the members of the crew. The Coxswain sits at the rear of the boat; but it is not the cox's responsibility to row, it is their responsibility to watch the stokes of the team, motivate the team when they are tiring, and monitor the progression of the boat during a race. The bow is seated at the front of the boat. The bow and seat two provide balance for the boat. With a smaller crew, the bow is the balance alone. If the bow is THE leader, he sits securely with his back towards the direction the boat is moving because he trusts his crew and trusts his Coxswain. Notice: I said if the bow is the leader. The United States Olympic Committee is not picking up an oar to join the race. They select the best crew; the best team, to represent the United States. So, I ask each leader, do you have enough confidence in your team and yourself to stand on land and watch your team represent you? Can you say to your team, "*I trust you?*"

References

"A Beginner's Guide to Rowing Crew." n.d. FitRated RSS. Accessed August 17, 2020. https://www.fitrated.com/beginners-guide-to-rowing-crew/

Alignment Media and Marketing, www.AlignmentMarketingAndMedia.com

Chand, Samuel, (Nov 2015) Tuesdays with Sam *Chand: The things that you can never delegate*

Duncan, Melba, (May 2011) The Case for Executive *Assistants. Harvard Business Review*

Gough, Martin. 2006. "How the Eight Works." BBC News. BBC. March 27, 2006. http://news.bbc.co.uk/sport2/hi/other_sports/rowing/4850246.stm.

"Meet the Teams." n.d. USRowing. Accessed August 17, 2020. https://usrowing.org/sports/2019/8/20/athlete- bios.aspx.

Rowingsoundsfun, R. (2012, December 09). Personality traits in an eight. Retrieved June 25, 2020, from https://rowingsoundsfun.tumblr.com/post/3750 3343446/personality-traits-in-an-eight

SoraNews24. (n.d.). 10 Japanese Business Etiquette Rules. Retrieved October 24, 2020, from https://allabout-japan.com/en/article/2695/2/

The Holy Bible New Living Translations; King James Version; New King James Version

"What Makes A Good Coxswain?" (2019, January 27). https://www.thecoxguide.com/what-makes-a-good-coxswain/

"When Clothing Style Influences Cognitive Style." 2015. May 8, 2015. https://www.psychologicalscience.org/news/minds-business/when-clothing-style-influences- cognitive-style.html.

Worldrowing. 2019. "Secret Training behind Rowing's Top Coxswains." April 8, 2019. http://www.worldrowing.com/news/secret- training-behind-rowing-top-coxswains.

About the Author

Michelle Small is a Certified Life Coach with over 30 years of corporate experience. This includes supporting C-Suite Executives, and as a programming engineer in engineer in Information Technology/ Telecommunications.

Michelle is an ordained minister, Teacher, Mentor, Entrepreneur and author. With a call to the faith-based sector, Michelle serves as a board member as the General Secretary for the Breath of Life Fellowship, Decatur Georgia.

In 2016, after receiving her certification a Life Coach from the "College of Social and Behavioral Science" in Brandon, Florida, Michelle formed Hagar's Hands, a 501c3 operating in the State of Georgia. Hagar's Hands provides training, career-pathing, and mentoring for executive assistants and those that support C-Suite Executives, both in the corporate and non-profit arenas. Known for her dynamic and pragmatic ability to equip and mobilize leaders. Her coaching style helps individuals discover their motivators, enabling them to develop a custom path that crosses all areas of one's life, career, family, and friendships.

Michelle also holds an associate degree in Religious Studies from "Tabernacle Bible College and Seminary," and currently, she is pursuing a Bachelor's Degree in Christian Leadership and Management from the Regent University. For more information, contact www.CourageousMi.com

Made in the USA
Columbia, SC
23 December 2020

28177300R00030